Lunch at the Zoo

by Brenda Cartee Lee

illustrated by Julia Sponsler

LITTLE COTTAGE BOOKS
Tallahassee, Florida

Copyright © 2003 by Brenda Cartee Lee
All rights reserved.
Little Cottage Books
Tallahassee, FL
www.littlecottagebooks.com

Library of Congress information
available upon request.

ISBN: 0-9728732-0-1

Designed by Carol Tornatore

Illustrated by Julia Sponsler

First Edition
1 2 3 4 5 6 7 8 9 10

Printed in China

This book is dedicated to
Mom and Dad Cartee,

(who **always** made me eat my vegetables)

and to Erica, Claire, Tres, Bayne
and Maggie

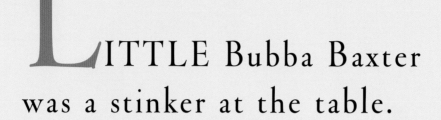

LITTLE Bubba Baxter
was a stinker at the table.

His mother fixed his breakfast
but he said he wasn't able.

Instead of eating cereal
with fruit piled up on top.

He wanted cake and ice cream
and a big red lollipop.

I'LL run away from home!" he cried.
"I'm going to the zoo."

"I'll run and play and laugh all day,
and eat what the animals do."

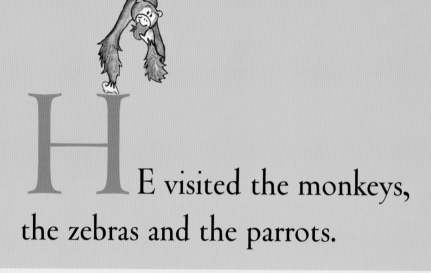

HE visited the monkeys,
the zebras and the parrots.

But they were eating peanuts,
apples, grains
And LOTS of carrots.

THE lions and the tigers,
Chase their prey on swift, strong feet.

But they eat chicken, pork and steak,
No JUNK and NOTHING sweet.

RACCOONS are soft and furry,
With black circles 'round their eyes.

But they eat corn and chicken eggs,
No candy, gum or pies.

THE wart hogs with their long,
brown snouts,
Eat roots from under trees.

But I wouldn't want to eat with them,
They eat on bended knees.

OH! There're the goats,
I can eat with them,
They run and play all day.

They'll eat most anything.
I'll have lunch with them today.

Goats are clever animals,
They climb the rocks with ease.

But when the lunch bell rings,
They eat bushes, grass and leaves.

THE gorilla is the King of Beasts.
I'll bet he gets HIS way.

But he eats berries and bananas,
Lots of fruit served on a tray.

THE owl's a wise old bird, he thought,
He sees from far and near.

But he eats mice and slippery snakes,

HEY . . . Get me out of here!

I LIKE the big, gray elephant,
I could eat there, I suppose.

But Mother wouldn't like it,
He picks food up with his nose.

PINK and white flamingos,
I can eat with them. (I'll beg.)

But they eat fish and water bugs,
While standing on one leg.

STICKS and stems are fine for goats,
And the owl can have his mouse,

But I'm a KID, I'M HUNGRY,
Now, I'm going to my house!

ALL of the animals in the zoo,
Are pretty, fast or strong,

No cake and ice cream on their plates,
No! That would be ALL wrong.

I'LL eat my fruits and vegetables,
The meats and all the rest.

I'm having lunch with MOM today,

MY MAMA KNOWS
WHAT'S BEST!

It may sound funny,
but healthy food is yummy!